We can all swim!

Written by Gill Munton

Speed Sounds

Consonants   *Ask children to say the sounds.*

f	l	m	n	r	s	v	z	**sh**	th	ng
ff	ll		nn		**ss**	ve	zz			**nk**
							s			

b	c	d	g	h	j	p	qu	t	w	x	y	ch
bb	k		gg					tt	wh			tch
	ck											

Each box contains one sound but sometimes more than one grapheme.
*Focus graphemes for this story are **circled**.*

Vowels

Ask children to say the sounds in and out of order.

a	e	i	o	u
at	hen	in	on	up

ay	ee	igh	ow	oo
day	see	high	blow	zoo

Story Green Words

Ask children to read the words first in Fred Talk and then say the word.

Ben   Jess   swim   tank   frog   pond   duck

Vocabulary Check

Discuss the meaning (as used in the non-fiction text) after the children have read the word.

big cat	definition a large, wild member of the cat family, e.g. a tiger

Red Words

Ask children to practise reading the words across the rows, down the columns and in and out of order clearly and quickly.

I	some	we
all	you	your
be	I	do
are	of	my

I am a fish. Fish can swim.
I can swim in a tank.

I am a frog.
Frogs can swim.

I can swim in a pond.

I am a duck. Ducks can swim.
I can swim on a pond.

I am a big cat.
Some big cats can swim.

I can swim.

I am Ben.
I can swim.

I am Jess.
I can swim.

We can all swim!

Can you swim?

16

Questions to talk about

Ask children to TTYP for each question using 'Fastest finger' (FF) or 'Have a think' (HaT).

p.9   (FF)   Where do some fish swim?

p.11   (FF)   Where do frogs swim?

p.13   (FF)   What sort of cats swim?

p.16   (FF)   Which other animals can swim?

Speedy Green Words

Ask children to practise reading the words across the rows, down the columns and in and out of order clearly and quickly.

am	fish	can
in	on	big
cat	am	fish
can	in	on

18